Published by Ice House Books

Planet Cat ® www.PlanetCatStudio.com

Copyright © 2019 Angie Rozelaar courtesy of Yellow House Art Licensing.

Illustrated by Angie Rozelaar

p9 Louno Morose / shutterstock.com
p11 vm2002 / shutterstock.com
p13 Oksana Mizina / shutterstock.com
p15 Stepanek Photography / shutterstock.com
p17 Brent Hofacker / shutterstock.com
p19 Alexander Prokopenko / shutterstock.com
p21 Brent Hofacker / shutterstock.com
p23 JeniFoto / shutterstock.com
p25 JeniFoto / shutterstock.com
p27 JeniFoto / shutterstock.com
p29 AlexeiLogvinovich / shutterstock.com
p31 kostrez / shutterstock.com
p33 AS Food studio / shutterstock.com
p35 Subbotina Anna / shutterstock.com

p37 nadianb / shutterstock.com
p39 minadezhda / shutterstock.com
p41 minadezhda / shutterstock.com
p43 Tatiana Volgutova / shutterstock.com
p45 Martin Gardeazabal / shutterstock.com
p47 Oksana Mizina / shutterstock.com
p49 Oksana Mizina / shutterstock.com
p51 Africa Studio / shutterstock.com
p53 Africa Studio / shutterstock.com
p55 Anna Shepulova / shutterstock.com
p57 Anna Shepulova / shutterstock.com
p59 istetiana / shutterstock.com
p61 istetiana / shutterstock.com

Ice House Books is an imprint of Half Moon Bay Limited
The Ice House, 124 Walcot Street, Bath, BA1 5BG
www.icehousebooks.co.uk

ISBN 978-1-912867-16-5

Printed in China

# FOOD FOR
# CRAZY CAT LADIES

ICE HOUSE BOOKS

# CONTENTS

# GUACOMOLE

## Ingredients

3 avocados
1 tomato
1 red onion
1 green chilli
juice from 1 lime
salt and pepper, to taste
sprig of coriander, for garnish
tortilla chips, to serve

Serves: 8
Prep time: 10 minutes

## Method

1. Cut the avocados in half and destone them. Scoop out the flesh and roughly chop it, then put it into a bowl and mash slightly with a fork.

2. Blanch, skin, deseed and finely chop the tomato. Finely chop the red onion, and deseed and finely chop the chilli. Add them all to the bowl of avocado.

3. Pour in the lime juice and season to taste with salt and pepper. Mix all the ingredients together well.

4. Serve the guacamole with a sprig of coriander and tortilla chips.

# TOMATO SALSA

## Ingredients

3 tbsp red onion
2 small garlic cloves
3 large tomatoes
1 green chilli
2 tbsp coriander
2 tbsp lime juice
salt and pepper, to taste

Serves: 6-8
Prep time: 15-20 minutes
Extra time: 2 hours chilling

## Method

1. Finely chop the onion and mince the garlic, then put into a strainer and add 450 ml (15 fl oz) of boiling water. Leave to drain and cool completely while you prepare the other ingredients.

2. Deseed and chop the tomatoes and chilli, then chop the coriander.

3. Add all the chopped ingredients to a bowl and pour in the lime juice. Stir well.

4. Pop the salsa in the fridge, for at least two hours, to blend the flavours. Season to taste with salt and pepper just before serving.

# PUMPKIN SOUP

## Ingredients

600 g (21 oz) pumpkin, peeled & deseeded
1 red onion, roughly chopped
1 garlic clove, crushed
1 tbsp olive oil
300 g (10½ oz) potatoes, peeled
500 ml (17½ fl oz) vegetable stock
salt and pepper, to taste
parsley, for garnish

Serves: 4
Prep time: 15–20 minutes
Cook time: 45–50 minutes

## Method

1. Preheat the oven to 200°C / 180°C fan / gas 6.

2. Cut the pumpkin into 1-inch cubes and spread out on a baking tray. Scatter over the onion and garlic, season well and drizzle over the oil. Roast in the oven for around 40 minutes (until soft).

3. While the pumpkin is in the oven, cube and boil the potatoes in a large pan over a medium heat for approx. eight minutes (until soft). Drain well.

4. Put the potatoes and roasted vegetables into a blender, along with the vegetable stock, and blend until totally smooth. (You may need to complete this step in a few batches.)

5. Pour the soup into a large pan and warm through before serving in bowls. Season to taste with salt and pepper, and garnish with fresh parsley.

# FRIED EGGS & VEGGiES

## Ingredients

400 g (14 oz) Brussels sprouts
3 tbsp olive oil
1 garlic clove, chopped
1 onion, chopped
150 g (5½ oz) chestnut mushrooms, sliced
salt and pepper, to taste
2 large free-range eggs
handful watercress

Serves: 2
Prep time: 10 minutes
Cook time: 25 minutes

## Method

1. Boil the Brussels sprouts in a medium pan for 10 minutes to soften them.

2. Pour the olive oil into a large frying pan and heat. Then add the chopped garlic and onion. Fry until the onion is cooked through.

3. Add the part-cooked Brussels sprouts and sliced mushroom to the pan and cook for a further five minutes, stirring occasionally.

4. Season well and fry until all the veggies are cooked how you like them.

5. Make two wells in the mixture and crack an egg into each one. Season again on top of the eggs and throw in the cress.

6. Once the eggs are cooked, spoon the mixture into two bowls and tuck in!

# SWEET POTATO FRiES

## Ingredients

900 g (32 oz) sweet potato, peeled
2 tbsp olive oil
1 tsp garlic powder
1 tsp paprika
salt and pepper, to taste

Serves: 4–6
Prep time: 10 minutes
Cook time: 25 minutes

## Method

1. Preheat the oven to 200°C / 180°C fan / gas 6.

2. Prepare the sweet potatoes by cutting them into sticks around three inches long and ¼-inch wide. Toss them in a large bowl with the oil.

3. In a small bowl, combine the garlic powder, paprika, and salt and pepper. Add the spices to the sweet potato fries and toss them together.

4. Put the fries onto two baking sheets and spread them out. Bake for approximately 15 minutes or until they have browned and are crisp on the bottom, then flip them and continue to bake until the other side is crisp (for around 10 minutes).

5. Serve with your favourite sauces!

# PEPPURR

# STUFFED PEPPERS

## Ingredients

1 tbsp olive oil
1 medium white onion, chopped
1 garlic clove, finely chopped
250 g (9 oz) beef or veggie mince
400 g (14 oz) tinned chopped tomatoes
1 beef or vegetable stock cube
1 tbsp tomato ketchup
16 oregano leaves
salt and pepper, to taste
2 large bell peppers
50 g (2 oz) grated cheddar cheese

Serves: 4
Prep time: 10 minutes
Cook time: 45 minutes

## Method

1. Preheat the oven to 200°C / 180°C fan / gas 6.

2. Heat the oil in a large pan over a medium heat. Add the onion and cook for approximately three minutes until softened. Add the garlic and mince, breaking up with a spoon, and cook until the mince has browned.

3. Stir in the tinned tomatoes, stock cube, ketchup and oregano. Season with salt and pepper, stir again, then cover the pan with a lid and leave the mix to simmer for 30 minutes.

4. While the mince mix is cooking, half the peppers and deseed them. Pop them in a roasting tin, cut-side up, and bake them for 20 minutes.

5. Once the mince is cooked, spoon it equally into the pepper halves. Sprinkle grated cheese on top and bake them in the oven for another 10 minutes. Allow to cool slightly before serving up.

PAWTATO

# BACON & CHEESE POTATO SKINS

## Ingredients

6 medium baking potatoes, halved
8 slices bacon, cooked and crumbled
55 g (2 oz) unsalted butter, melted
salt and pepper, to taste
250 g (9 oz) grated cheddar cheese
sour cream, for garnish
spring onion, chopped, for garnish

Serves: 6-10
Prep time: 30 minutes
Cook time: 1 hour and 15 minutes

## Method

1. Preheat the oven to 200°C / 180°C fan / gas 6.

2. Prick the potatoes with a fork and put them on a baking sheet. Bake for one hour and leave them to cool for at least 15 minutes when they come out of the oven.

3. Cut the potatoes in half lengthwise and scoop out most of the potato in the middle, leaving a layer of potato near the skin.

4. Put the potato inners in a bowl and mix with your cooked and crumbled bacon. Set aside for now.

5. Brush the inside and outside of the potato skins with the melted butter and season with salt and pepper. Pop them back in the oven for approximately 7-8 minutes (until the insides are crispy).

6. Remove the skins from the oven and fill them with your potato and bacon mix. Top them with the grated cheese and bake again for three minutes – or until the cheese is bubbling nicely.

7. Top with a dollop of sour cream and chopped spring onion to serve.

# MUSHROOM, CHICKEN & SPINACH GNOCCHI

## Ingredients

1-2 tbsp olive oil

450 g (16 oz) boneless and skinless chicken,
cut into bite-sized chunks (or veggie alternative)

150 g (5 oz) mushrooms (½ sliced, ½ finely chopped)

1 white onion, finely chopped

½ garlic clove, finely chopped

100 g (3½ oz) unsalted butter

100 g (3½ oz) plain flour

700 ml (24 fl oz) milk

475 ml (16 fl oz) chicken or vegetable stock

120 ml (4 fl oz) double cream

100 g (3½ oz) cream cheese

500 g (17½ oz) potato gnocchi

900 g (32 oz) baby spinach

salt and pepper, to taste

Serves: 6-8
Prep time: 10 minutes
Cook time: 30-35 minutes

Turn the page for the method...

# Method

1. Heat a tablespoon of oil in a large pan over a medium-high heat. Once warm, add the chicken and half of the mushrooms (sliced). Cook until the chicken has no pink remaining and is fully cooked through. Set the chicken and mushrooms aside in a covered bowl.

2. In the same pan, still over a medium-high heat, add the finely chopped onion, garlic and mushrooms. Cook them for around two minutes, until they start to brown.

3. Add the butter to the pan with the onion mixture and allow it to melt, then stir in the plain flour until well mixed. Pour in the milk gradually, whisking constantly to remove lumps as the sauce thickens.

4. Gradually add the stock in the same way you added the milk, constantly mixing to prevent lumps. The sauce should be creamy and thick.

5. Reduce the heat and add the double cream and cream cheese to the sauce. Gently stir until the cream cheese has melted.

6. Meanwhile, bring a pan of water to the boil, then drop in the gnocchi. Leave for one minute then drain.

7. Add the gnocchi, spinach, and the chicken and mushroom mix to the sauce. Stir until the spinach has wilted and everything is warmed through. Season with salt and pepper and serve hot.

WATERMEOWLON

# SUMMER SALAD

## Ingredients

green salad leaves, torn
1 small seedless watermelon, cubed
2 large tomatoes, wedges
8 cherry tomatoes, halved
½ red onion, sliced
75 g (2½ oz) feta cheese, crumbled
drizzle olive oil
drizzle white balsamic vinegar
salt and pepper, to taste

Serves: 4
Prep time: 10 minutes

## Method

1. Arrange the salad leaves on the plate.

2. In a large bowl, add the watermelon, tomatoes, red onion and feta. Gently mix them.

3. Drizzle over some olive oil and white balsamic vinegar, then season with salt and pepper. Give the salad another mix then serve over the salad leaves.

PURRNAPPLE

# GRILLED PINEAPPLE

## Ingredients

1 large pineapple
1–3 tbsp honey, to taste
2–3 tbsp butter, melted
1 tbsp lemon juice
mint leaves, for garnish

Makes: several rings
Prep time: 10 minutes
Cook time: 10 minutes

## Method

1. Trim the top off the pineapple then core and peel it. Cut the flesh into ring slices, approximately one inch thick.

2. In a small bowl, stir the honey, butter, and lemon juice together.

3. Brush the honey glaze onto both sides of the pineapple rings.

4. Heat a ridged cast-iron griddle pan on the hob until very hot. Grill the pineapple for a couple of minutes on each side, or until the sugar caramelizes, leaving grill marks.

5. Brush over any remaining honey glaze. Serve with mint leaves for garnish.

# STRAWPURRY

# STRAWBERRY JAM

## Ingredients

600 g (21 oz) strawberries
juice of one lemon
600 g (21 oz) jam sugar

Makes: 6 jars (approx.)
Prep time: 20 minutes
Cook time: 20 minutes
Extra time: 12 hours cooling

## Method

1. First, sterilise your jars. Heat the oven to 120°C / 100°C fan / gas ½. Place your clean jars on a baking tray with space in between them. Put them in the oven for 20 minutes then turn off the heat, but leave the jars in the oven keeping warm until the jam is ready. Also put a small plate in the fridge to chill.

2. Wash your strawberries, remove the stems and chop them into quarters. Place them into a large saucepan, add the lemon juice and mix until well combined.

3. On a low heat, cook the fruit until it is completely soft, then carefully add the sugar, stirring to dissolve.

4. Once all the sugar has dissolved, increase the heat and cook on a steady boil until the setting point is reached. To test your jam, spoon a little onto your chilled plate, wait for it to cool and push it with your finger – when the jam is set the surface should crinkle.

5. Take the jam off the heat and allow to sit for a few minutes before packing into jars – this should prevent all the pieces of fruit floating to the top. Put on the lids while the jam is still hot to create a seal. Closed jars kept in a cool, dark place will last one year. Once opened, keep in the fridge for up to two weeks.

# MARMALADE MUFFINS

## Ingredients

175 g (6 oz) plain flour
25 g (1 oz) porridge oats
175 g (6 oz) soft light brown sugar
1 tsp baking powder
½ tsp bicarbonate of soda
zest and juice from 1 orange
1 tbsp sunflower oil
150 g (5 oz) pot plain yoghurt
1 large free-range egg
9 tsp chunky marmalade
handful of sultanas

Makes: 9 muffins
Prep time: 15 minutes
Cook time: 15 minutes

## Method

1. Line a muffin tin with nine paper cases and heat your oven to 200°C / 180°C fan / gas 6. In a large bowl, mix the flour, oats, sugar, baking powder and bicarbonate of soda.

2. In a separate bowl, whisk together the orange zest and juice, oil, yoghurt and egg, then lightly stir into the flour mixture until just combined.

3. Spoon one tablespoon of the mixture into each muffin case. Layer with one tablespoon of marmalade and add a few sultanas, then add more muffin mixture until the cases are two thirds full.

4. Bake for 15–20 minutes until golden on top and a skewer comes out clean. Leave to cool slightly, then enjoy!

# BLUEBERRY PANCAKES

## Ingredients

135 g (5 oz) plain flour
1 tsp baking powder
½ tsp salt
2 tbsp caster sugar
1 free-range egg
130 ml (4½ fl oz) milk
2 tbsp melted butter, cooled
1–2 knobs of butter

maple syrup, fresh blueberries
and fresh mint to serve

Serves: 3–4
Prep time: 30 minutes
Cook time: 30 minutes (approx.)

Turn the page for the method ...

# Method

1. Start by sifting the flour, baking powder, salt and caster sugar into a large mixing bowl. Mix well.

2. In a separate bowl, whisk the egg and milk together then add the melted butter and whisk again.

3. Add the wet ingredients to the dry ingredients and beat until the batter is smooth. Leave the batter to stand for 20 minutes before making your pancakes.

4. Heat a frying pan over a medium heat. When the pan is warm, add a knob of butter and wait for it to melt.

5. Pour in enough batter to form a small, thick circle per pancake and cook until the tops start to bubble. Flip each pancake over and cook until both sides are golden brown. You can probably cook three pancakes at a time.

6. Serve the pancakes in stacks with a drizzle of maple syrup, topped with blueberries and fresh mint.

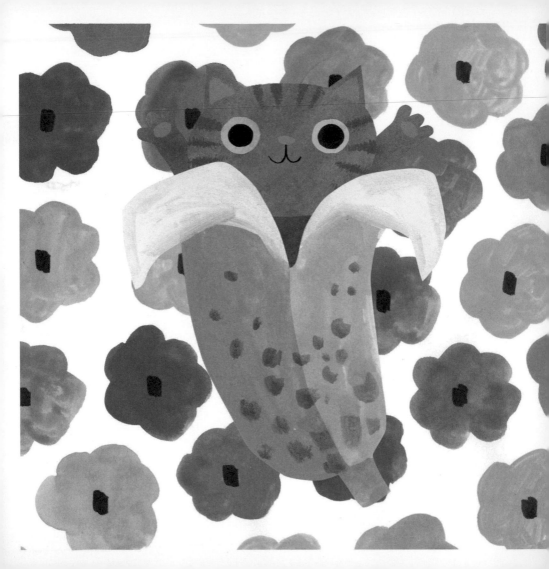

# BANANA BREAD

## Ingredients

285 g (10 oz) plain flour
1 tsp bicarbonate of soda
½ tsp salt
110 g (4 oz) butter, room temp
225 g (8 oz) caster sugar
2 free-range eggs
4 bananas, mashed
85 ml (3 fl oz) buttermilk
1 tsp vanilla extract

Serves: 10
Prep time: 20 minutes
Cook time: 1 hour

Turn the page for the method...

## Method

1. Preheat the oven to 180°C / 160°C fan / gas 4 and prepare a loaf tin by greasing it with a little butter.

2. In a large mixing bowl, sift in the flour, bicarbonate or soda, and salt and give them a stir.

3. Beat the butter and sugar together in a different mixing bowl, until light and fluffy.

4. Add the eggs, one at a time, along with the mashed bananas, buttermilk, and vanilla extract, to the butter mix. Mix them in well then fold in the dry ingredients and mix until just combined.

5. Pour the cake batter into the greased loaf tin and pop it in the oven. Bake for approximately one hour or until the banana bread is golden-brown on top and has risen.

6. Leave the banana bread to cool a little before transferring it to a wire rack to cool completely. Enjoy with a cuppa!

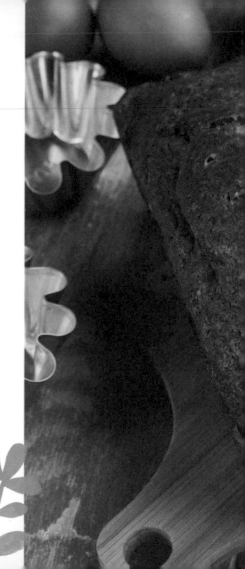

# PEACH SORBET

## Ingredients

4 medium peaches, sliced
1 tbsp honey
1 tsp lemon juice
60 ml (2 fl oz) warm water,
as needed
fresh peach slices, to serve
fresh mint, for garnish

Serves: 4
Prep time: 20 minutes
Extra time: 3-4 hours for freezing

## Method

1. Line a baking sheet with greaseproof paper. Slice the peaches and remove the pit, then line up the peach slices on the baking sheet.

2. Pop the peach slices into the freezer and leave them until they're completely solid (approximately 3-4 hours).

3. Put the frozen peach slices into a food processor, along with the honey and lemon juice, and blend until smooth. If the sorbet is very stiff, add some warm water to help loosen it a little.

4. Serve straight away with fresh mint and peach slices, or freeze if you prefer it firm.

# CHOCOLATE-CHIP COOKIES

## Ingredients

150 g (5 oz) salted butter, room temp
80 g (3 oz) light brown muscovado sugar
80 g (3 oz) granulated sugar
1 free-range egg
2 tsp vanilla extract
225 g (8 oz) plain flour
½ tsp bicarbonate of soda
¼ tsp salt
200 g (7 oz) milk chocolate chips

Makes: 30 cookies (approx.)
Prep time: 15 minutes
Cook time: 8–10 minutes

## Method

1. Preheat the oven to 190°C / 170°C fan / gas 5 and prepare two baking sheets by lining them with greaseproof paper.

2. In a large mixing bowl, beat the butter and two sugars together until creamy. Add the egg and vanilla extract and continue to beat until combined.

3. Sift the flour, bicarbonate of soda and salt into a separate mixing bowl and mix.

4. Add the dry ingredients to the wet ingredients and mix until just combined. Pour in the chocolate chips and stir until they are nicely spread throughout the dough.

5. Spoon the cookie dough onto the baking sheets, leaving space between each cookie because they will spread during baking. If you use a teaspoon, this mixture will make around 30 cookies.

6. Bake for 8–10 minutes until the edges turn golden. Leave them to cool slightly on the baking sheets before transferring them to a wire rack to cool completely.

SOURPUSS

# LEMON CHEESECAKE

## Ingredients

For the base:
430 g (15 oz) digestive biscuits
100 g (3½ oz) unsalted butter, melted

For the filling:
300 ml (10 fl oz) double cream
60 g (2 oz) icing sugar
450 g (16 oz) soft cheese, room temp
100 g (3½ oz) caster sugar
120 g (4 oz) lemon curd
zest from 1 lemon
lemon slices, for garnish
mint leaves, for garnish

Serves: 8-10
Prep time: 30 minutes
Extra time: 4-6 hours chilling

Turn the page for the method...

# Method

1. Line the bottom of a 9-inch round, loose-bottom cake tin with greaseproof paper and grease the sides with a little butter.

2. Crush the biscuits into fine crumbs – either by putting them into a plastic bag and using a rolling pin to bash them, or by putting them into a food processor. Tip the biscuit crumbs into a large bowl.

3. Put the butter into a small bowl and melt it in the microwave for 30–45 seconds. Pour the butter over the biscuit crumbs and mix until the crumbs are coated.

4. Carefully pour the biscuit crumbs into the cake tin. Firmly press them into the bottom and up the sides of the tin to create a thick biscuit crust.

5. Chill a large bowl in the freezer for approx. 10 minutes. Once chilled, pour in the double cream and whip it using an electric mixer until the cream begins to thicken. Gradually add the icing sugar. Continue to beat until soft peaks form, then set the bowl aside.

6. In another bowl, beat the soft cheese until smooth. Add the caster sugar and beat again until smooth. Add the lemon curd and zest and continue to beat until combined and smooth.

7. Fold the whipped double cream into the cream cheese mixture and stir until combined. Pour the filling onto the biscuit base and carefully spread it out so it's even.

8. Pop your cheesecake in the fridge for 4–6 hours until set. Serve with lemon slices and fresh mint on top.

# PARTY CUPCAKES

## Ingredients

For the cupcakes:
175 g (6 oz) butter, room temp
175 g (6 oz) caster sugar
175 g (6 oz) self-raising flour
½ tsp baking powder
3 free-range eggs
1 tsp vanilla extract

For the buttercream:
175 g (6 oz) butter, room temp
350 g (12 oz) icing sugar
½ tsp vanilla extract
pink or red edible food colouring
1 tbsp milk (if needed)

Serves: 12
Prep time: 15 minutes
Cook time: 20–25 minutes

## Method

1. Preheat the oven to 180°C / 160°C fan / gas 4 and line a 12-hole cupcake tin with paper cases.

2. In a mixing bowl, add the butter and sugar and cream them together until smooth. Sift in the flour and baking powder and give the ingredients a good mix, then add the eggs and vanilla extract and continue to mix until combined.

Method continued on the next page ...

3. Spoon the mixture into the cupcake cases so they are two thirds full. Pop them in the oven and bake for 20–25 minutes or until the cupcakes have risen. Use a skewer to test the cupcakes are baked all the way through – if the skewer comes out clean, they're baked. Leave to cool on a wire rack.

4. While the cupcakes are baking and cooling, you can make the buttercream icing. Beat the butter until pale, sift in the icing sugar and continue to beat. Add the vanilla extract and food colouring (add a little colouring at a time to ensure you get the effect you want) and mix everything together. If the buttercream is stiff, add one tablespoon of milk and mix again.

5. Spoon the buttercream into a piping bag fitted with a star nozzle and pipe on your buttercream swirl (wait until the cupcakes have cooled before decorating).

6. Serve up at your next party!

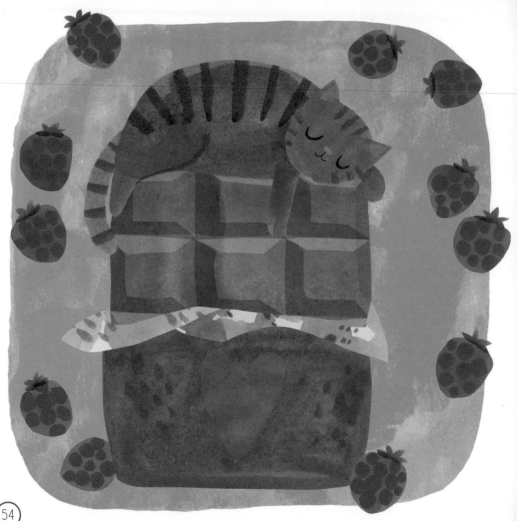

# CHOCOLATE & RASPBERRY BROWNIES

## Ingredients

200 g (7 oz) dark chocolate, chunks
100 g (3½ oz) milk chocolate, chunks
250 g (9 oz) unsalted butter
400 g (14 oz) soft light brown sugar
4 free-range eggs
140 g (5 oz) plain flour
50 g (2 oz) cocoa powder
200 g (7 oz) raspberries

Serves: 15
Prep time: 15-20 minutes
Cook time: 30 minutes

Turn the page for the method ...

# Method

1. Preheat the oven to 180°C / 160°C fan / gas 4 and line a baking tray with greaseproof paper (we recommened a 20cm x 30cm baking tray).

2. Heat a large pan over a low heat and add the dark and milk chocolate, butter and sugar. Gently melt them and stir occasionally with a wooden spoon. Once melted, remove the pan from the heat.

3. Add the eggs to the chocolate mixture, one at a time, and stir them in.

4. Sift in the flour and cocoa powder and stir again, then stir in half of the raspberries.

5. Pour the brownie mix into the baking tray and scatter over the remaining raspberries. Bake for approximately 30 minutes.

6. Leave the brownie to cool before slicing it into squares. Dust over a little cocoa powder and garnish with fresh raspberries.

# PURR-SHAPED

# PEAR & BLACKBERRY CRUMBLE

## Ingredients

For the topping:
110 g (4 oz) butter, room temp
180 g (6 oz) plain flour
110 g (4 oz) demerara sugar

For the filling:
5 pears, peeled
150 g (5 oz) caster sugar
300 g (10½ oz) blackberries

Makes: 4-6 servings
Prep time: 20-30 minutes
Cook time: 35-40 minutes

Turn the page for the method . . .

# Method

1. Preheat the oven to 180°C / 160°C fan / gas 4 and grease an ovenproof dish with a little butter.

2. Begin by making the crumble topping. Cut the butter into cubes and combine it with the flour in a large mixing bowl, using your fingertips. Mix until it looks like breadcrumbs. Add the sugar and continue to mix until combined. Set aside.

3. To make the filling, put the whole pears into a large pan and pour over water until they're covered. Add 50 g (1.7 oz) of the sugar and bring to the boil. Reduce the heat to a simmer and cook until the pears are tender, for around 10–12 minutes. Drain the mixture and leave the pears to cool.

4. Once the pears have cooled, remove their cores and finely chop the flesh.

5. Spoon approximately one quarter of the pears into the prepared dish so there's an even layer at the bottom. Top with one quarter of the blackberries and sprinkle over two tablespoons of the sugar. Continue layering like this until all of the pears, blackberries and sugar have been used.

6. Top the pear and blackberries with the crumble mixture. Bake for approximately 20–25 minutes or until the crumble is golden-brown.

7. Serve with a helping of custard or cream!